W9-AIJ-203

Pebble® Plus

Nocturnal Animals

Porcupines

by Mary R. Dunn

Consulting Editor: Gail Saunders-Smith, PhD

Consultant: Tanya Dewey, PhD
University of Michigan Museum of Zoology

CAPSTONE PRESS
a capstone imprint

Pebble Plus is published by Capstone Press,
151 Good Counsel Drive, P.O. Box 669, Mankato, Minnesota 56002.
www.capstonepub.com

Copyright © 2011 by Capstone Press, a Capstone imprint. All rights reserved.
No part of this publication may be reproduced in whole or in part, or stored in a retrieval system, or transmitted in any
form or by any means, electronic, mechanical, photocopying, recording, or otherwise, without written permission of the
publisher. For information regarding permission, write to Capstone Press,
151 Good Counsel Drive, P.O. Box 669, Dept. R, Mankato, Minnesota 56002.

Books published by Capstone Press are manufactured with paper
containing at least 10 percent post-consumer waste.

Library of Congress Cataloging-in-Publication Data
Dunn, Mary R.
  Porcupines / by Mary R. Dunn.
      p. cm. — (Pebble plus. Nocturnal animals)
  Includes bibliographical references and index.
  Summary: "Simple text and full-color photos explain the habitat, life cycle, range, and behavior of porcupines"—
Provided by publisher.
  ISBN 978-1-4296-5289-6 (library binding)
  ISBN 978-1-4296-6193-5 (paperback)
  1. Porcupines—Juvenile literature. I. Title. II. Series.
QL737.R652D86 2011
599.35'97—dc22   2010028681

Editorial Credits

Katy Kudela, editor; Ashlee Suker, designer; Marcie Spence, media researcher; Laura Manthe, production specialist

Photo Credits

Alamy Images: Martin Harvey, cover; iStockphoto: oneword, 15; Minden Pictures: Mark Moffett, 21; Peter Arnold, Inc.:
Martin Harvey, 7; Shutterstock: Condor 36, 13, Lynsey Allen, 9, Tony Rix, 1; SuperStock: All Canada Photos, 17; Visuals
Unlimited: Cheryl Ertelt, 5, Dave Watts, 11, Gerald & Buff Corsi, 19

Note to Parents and Teachers

The Nocturnal Animals series supports national science standards related to life science.
This book describes and illustrates porcupines. The images support early readers in
understanding the text. The repetition of words and phrases helps early readers learn new
words. This book also introduces early readers to subject-specific vocabulary words, which are
defined in the Glossary section. Early readers may need assistance to read some words and to
use the Table of Contents, Glossary, Read More, Internet Sites, and Index sections of the book.

Printed in the United States of America in North Mankato, Minnesota.
092010
005933CGS11

Table of Contents

Prickly Prowlers

Spiky porcupines nap during the day. But these nocturnal animals wake up at night. They waddle through their forest homes.

There are 27 kinds of porcupines found around the world. Most porcupines live alone. Some live in family groups.

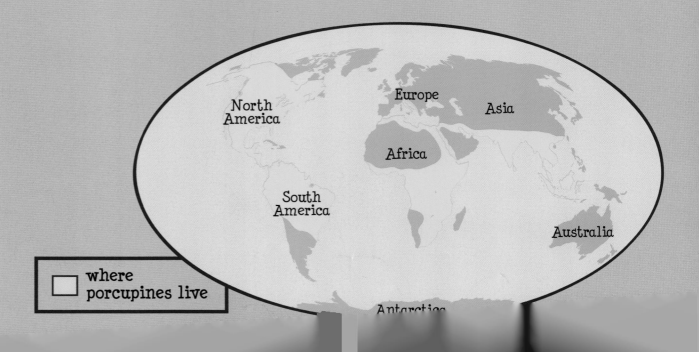

where porcupines live

North America

Europe

Asia

Africa

South America

Australia

Antarctica

Up Close!

Most porcupines have stocky bodies with sharp quills covering them from head to tail. As adults, porcupines can weigh up to 66 pounds (30 kilograms).

Porcupines have an
excellent sense of smell.

They sniff for food in the dark.

They sniff the air to find out
if predators are near.

Some porcupines are tree climbers. These porcupines use their long, sharp claws to dig into tree bark.

Finding Food

Porcupines use their

long front teeth

to chomp on twigs and roots.

They also eat leaves and fruits.

Growing Up

Once or twice a year, females
have soft-quilled porcupettes.
Mothers keep their young safe.
They teach their young
to find food.

Staying Safe

When in danger

porcupines lash their tails.

They raise their sharp quills.

Watch out! Predators that get

close will get stuck with quills.

Porcupines listen for danger.

They stay away from

owls and other predators.

Porcupines that stay safe

can live up to 18 years.

Glossary

chomp—to chew or bite something

lash—to whip back and forth

nocturnal—happening at night; a nocturnal animal is active at night

porcupette—a young porcupine

predator—an animal that hunts other animals for food

quill—a long, pointed spine

stocky—short and heavy

waddle—to walk taking short steps and swaying from side to side

Read More

Nichols, Catherine. *Prickly Porcupines*. Gross-Out Defenses. New York: Bearport Pub., 2009.

Ripple, William John. *Porcupines*. Woodland Animals. Mankato, Minn.: Capstone Press, 2006.

Internet Sites

FactHound offers a safe, fun way to find Internet sites related to this book. All of the sites on FactHound have been researched by our staff.

Here's all you do:

Visit *www.facthound.com*

Type in this code: 9781429652896

 Check out projects, games and lots more at
www.capstonekids.com

Index

Word Count: 190
Grade: 1
Early-Intervention Level: 17